My Gift to You

This book is presented as a Gift to:

_____

From:

_____

Date:

_____

Live life with valor and make a difference!

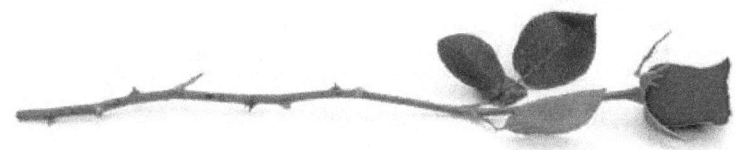

I am Beautiful!

Tell yourself every morning. Smile and spread love everywhere your journey takes you. Let no heart leave your presence feeling untouched.

Good Morning Me

Good Morning me, how was our rest last night?
We have a great day ahead of us if we don't lose sight.
Did we get up on the right or wrong side of the bed?
Are good thoughts or bad running through our head?
As I look in the mirror, here's what I see,
A beautiful person inside and out and in you I believe.
We will empower others today so they too can achieve,
To make our world better so that all can receive.

*When you empower others,
you make the world better around you.*

© J. B. Love

Love, Life & Courage
(Poetry for the Soul)

by
J. B. Love

Good Morning Me and *Win Big by Choosing Right (modified from Choices)* poems where taken from *Anticipation, 10 Keys to Turning Your Dreams into Reality* @2010 by J. B. Love

The Scripture quotation in the conclusion was taken from the *King James Version* of the *Bible*.

©2010, 2015 and 2016 by J. B. Love.

Library of Congress Control Number   2016901498
J. B. Love Books, Jackson, Mississippi

ISBN: Softcover   978-0-9971875-0-2
                 E-book   978-0-9971875-1-9

All rights reserved. No part of this book may be reproduced or transmitted in any form or by any means, electronically or mechanically including photocopying, recording or by any information storage devices or retrieval systems without permission in writing from the copyright owner, except in the case of brief quotations embodied in critical reviews and certain other noncommercial uses permitted by copyright law. For permission requests, write to the publisher, addressed "Attention: Permissions Coordinator," at the address below:

J. B. Love Books
P. O. Box 10801
Jackson, MS 39289
www.jblovebooks.com

This book was printed in the United States of America

Contents

Acknowledgment 7
Dedication 9
Introduction *(A Story to Tell)* 11

Part 1: Love 13-15

My Dream Wish 16
Visions 17
Loneliness 18
Remembering Love *(A Tribute to My Teddy)* 19
Two Hearts 20
Your Sweetness 21
My Everything 22
Safe Haven 23
Forbidden Love 24
Emotional Struggle 25
You are the One 26
Still 27
Inspiration *(A Tribute to a Legend)* 28
God's Love *(A Song of Love)* 29
A Mother's Love is Always 30
Reflections of Love *(A Tribute to Momma)* 31
Grateful Love *(A Grandmother Who Was Heaven Sent)* 32
Thank You 32
Romance Departed 33
Broken Promises of Love 34
Learning to Love Me 35
The Magic in You 35
Why I am Beautiful 36
Beauty Undefined 37
Love Is 38
Love is Not 39
Too Educated to Quit 39
Love versus Lust 40-41
Win Big by Choosing Right 41
Joy Comes in the Morning *(A Love Letter to My Heart)* 42
The Sun Shall Always Rise 43
Better 44
Unstoppable Love Share 45

Part 2: Life and Courage 47-49

Life in Motion	50
The Cycle of Life *(Born to Live)*	51
To Live or Not	52
Life is Like a Poem	53
Courage Is	54
The Courage to Rise	55
The Courage to Begin	56
The Courage to Live	57
Daybreak *(A Chance to Start Out New)*	58
Paradise	59
Remembering When *(A Tribute to Grandma)*	60-61
I Say	62
A Mind of Many Colors	63
One Sistah's Cry	64
My Essence	65
Fence Riders	66
A Fair-Weather Friend	67
Modified Serenity Prayer	67
A Vow of Silence	68
In the Middle	69
Why Bother	70
Who am I?	71
Bless the Little Children	72
Because of You *(A Child's Plea)*	73
I See, I Hear, I Do	74
Grind to Shine	74
Move, Grove and Be You	75
Change Begins with Me	76-77
Be a Blessing Everyday	77
Encouraged	78
The House of They	79
Conclusion	81
A Hater's Prayer	81

Acknowledgment

*To all that have provided inspiration and/or made this project possible
I Acknowledge You*

Grind to Shine photo designed by Freepik

(My heart feels you Andrew, Michael & Vickie)

Live life with valor

```
      L
   COURAGE
      V
   LIFE
```

LOVE, LIFE & COURAGE

Dedication

This book of poetry is dedicated to:

- My loving husband, Michael, who I affectionately refer to as BAE and Teddy. Without his inspiration, this could not have been possible.

- In loving memory of my brother, Timothy – *Sometimes I would fantasize that if I had one wish I would want to make you well again. Maybe all wishes are not fantasies because I know our God does answer prayers. Thanks for the smiles. They were always a constant source of light in my world growing up.*

- The children, women and men I have assisted in child abuse and domestic violence situations.

Above all, I am grateful to God, who has given me the ability to express myself through words. I keep receiving blessings daily. I am thankful to have wonderful parents, Carl, and Earie, and I am also indebted to my many family members and friends who encouraged me along the way. I cannot thank them all enough. To all of the above I dedicate the following verse:

My Colorful World

A world without you would be a world without color.
May you continue to inspire me to paint my world a masterpiece.

Live life with valor

```
    L
    O
COURAGE
    V
    E
  LIFE
```

LOVE, LIFE & COURAGE

Introduction

A Story to Tell

I'm back with my sophomore project, *Love, Life & Courage (Poetry for the Soul)*. I hope you enjoyed *Anticipation—10 Keys to Turning Your Dreams into Reality*. I have a story to tell, and it is one of love, life and courage. I wrote it from my heart, and it consists of poems that are the results of my experiences and observations with these three elements of living. What connected these elements together for me was my valor *(personal bravery)*. The personal bravery to love, to live life to its fullest on my terms, and to be courageous.

Love, Life & Courage is more than just your average poetry book. It tells the story of my journey through life. Through the use of poems, you will be taken on a journey of discovery that will lead you to find yourself and to invoke a sense of responsibility to yourself and others to take the necessary steps toward living your life to its fullest on your terms. The poems in this book take a look at love, the challenges we all go through in life, and examines what it means to be courageous. Part I of this book focuses on Love. The love poems were poems that I wrote for my husband when we were dating, and he was in the military on deployment in foreign waters and after we were married. He kept them over the years. From time to time, I read them and am reminded of those feelings that help change my life. The poems that focus on the love that was departed and me learning to love myself are from a past relationship. My heart often reminds me of my mother and father, grandmother, and God's love that helped shape my life and the magic of strangers' bravery, smile and kind heart that unknowingly to them gave me the courage to face a difficult task. Since then unknowingly I have had the same effect on others. Part II focuses on life and courage. It is my participation in this thing called life and my observations of abuse; especially child abuse and the silence that served as a catalyst for continued violence against its victims. This book was written to help and inspire you to become a better you.

Live life with valor

```
        L
   COURAGE
        V
    LIFE
```

LOVE, LIFE & COURAGE

Part 1: Love

To love and to be loved is truly rewarding. Some people live their whole life feeling they have never experienced either. If you have never been in love, I hope you can take advantage of the knowledge and imagine yourself at the place and time these words of heartfelt emotions will take you. To love also means learning to love yourself. Without loving yourself, self-esteem cannot exist, and you cannot give love to others. People cannot give what they do not possess. The poems in this book inspired me write *How to Find, Enjoy and Keep Real Love (A Common Sense Guide to a Healthy Relationship)*. Once in a lifetime life throws you a fairytale of love. Will you be ready when opportunity knocks? It helps to prepare you for that journey of your heart falling so that you can rise in love with the right person.

I have used the red rose as a symbol of love, life and courage in this collection of poetry. For as long as I can remember it has been the most popular way to say "I Love You." You probably wished at some point in your life to receive a dozen or two on that special occasion. According to WebExhibits.org, in Greek mythology, the red rose was a symbol for the cycle of growth and decay *(life)*, but also for love and affinity. The rose itself have prickles that we call thorns that are quite bothersome to growers, yet it has the courage to produce a flower that is so beautiful. Just like the rose, you too can have the courage to show love, to be loved, and to live life to its fullest on your terms. The valor *(personal bravery)* you need resides within you. It will make you a better you. In my book, *Anticipation: 10 Keys to Turning Your Dreams into Reality* I asked the question: Who's on your DREAM TEAM? I hope the answer to this question was people who uplift you; otherwise, you need to rid negativity from your space because it hinders growth. Among the people that uplift you should be a mate that loves you more than you love yourself. If you have this type of partner on your DREAM TEAM, the rest of life's challenges will be easier.

J. B. LOVE

Live life with valor

```
        L
COURAGE
        V
    LIFE
```

LOVE, LIFE & COURAGE

Out of the ashes of despair, I learned to love myself and what emerged was a beautiful woman inside and out with a different walk. I know a thing or two about overcoming obstacles. I am a breast cancer and domestic violence survivor from an attempt on my life. Learning to love after this was tough for me at first, but I did it. You can do it too. In the midst of darkness, the light is always there. You just need to find it. The secret is the majority of the time that light is within you. Often we cannot find it because the haze from too much negativity smothers our glow. Removing negative energy from your space is the most important investment you will ever make in yourself. It gets rid of the haze, and now you can begin to shine. Your glow will attract others when they see it shining brightly. Sometimes life throws you lemons, and you must make lemonade to survive and start living again. I am better. I live better and love better and so can you.

Loving yourself also means taking care of yourself. Sometimes we give less attention to ourselves than we do others. Here is my self-care regimen that helps me stay healthy: I rid negativity from my space to reduce stress. I get plenty of sleep. I drink plenty of fluids; especially water. I eat healthily. I exercise. I get regular medical check-ups. I am living proof that early detection help saves lives. I meditate, pray and listen to music as it helps heals my soul. I have fun. I dream, but I live in reality, take action and keep a positive attitude. I smile, empower others and share love. There is no greater satisfaction. I am not saying you should follow my regimen. I mean you should have one. You should consult your doctor to ensure your regimen is healthy for you. If you are reading this and you have not had a medical exam in years or since you've been an adult, STOP NOW and MAKE a CALL for an appointment or visit your local free clinic.

Can you remember the time when you first fell in love, and it was real? Who was it? Where were you and what were you were doing? You should not confuse this with lust as lust and love are two different things. Maybe you can remember when love was absence or a mother's love. Do you need to learn to love yourself? What about when love is forbidden or the love you received just because it was Monday, Tuesday, Wednesday, Thursday, Friday, Saturday or Sunday? Let's turn the pages and take a look at my experiences and observations of LOVE.

Live life with valor

My Dream Wish

I had a dream or was it reality?
Someone so sweet and kind came into my life.
Can this be real? This man is too good to me.

This must be a dream.
Will I awaken with only a faint memory,
Or will I sleep and dream forever,
Of a prince charming too good to be?

We talk, we laugh, and sometimes I shed a tear,
Longing for my prince,
Wishing he were here.

If it is only a dream, I hope I sleep forever.
We have so much in common this prince and I.
If it is truly real, I wish we will always be together.

This is my dream wish.
It is what I truly feel.
This is too good to be a dream;
Therefore, it must be real.

Dreams can and do turn into realities with the right actions.

LOVE, LIFE & COURAGE

Vision

Across the miles, I see a vision,
A figure so bright and strong.
Bright like the sun, which sends the clouds away.
Strong like the Arctic winds, which blows each and every day.

Over the sea, my vision speaks to me,
Whispering to me to come closer, you have nothing to fear.
It is as though this vision is really real,
As it draws nearer and nearer.

Maybe it is just my imagination playing tricks on me,
Or maybe it is only the sun,
Glistening through the forest trees,
To wrap me in its warm arms.

Whatever it is, it seems always to be there,
Still brighter and stronger than ever,
Protecting me from harm,
Showering me with care.

I feel your presence when you're not here.

J. B. LOVE

Live life with valor

Loneliness

Days go by as I think of you,
Hoping that your love for me is still true.

Light turns into dark here in my empty nest,
Wondering where you are as I lay my head to rest.

Memories still linger of things we shared when you were here,
Reaching out to touch you, but you are not there.

Seconds become minutes as I'm so alone and feeling blue,
Filling my world with emptiness, without you.

Forever turned into now, oh how I miss my tomorrow,
Looking for peace as I work through my pain and sorrow.

Teardrops cascade into rivers as I search in the dark for my light.
You had become my sun and my onliness,
And now my heart is filled with so much loneliness.

Forever turns into now when you're absent from my arms.

LOVE, LIFE & COURAGE

Remembering Love
(A Tribute to My Teddy)

Walking barefoot on the beach, we felt the warmth of the sand.
Strolling through the park, we were always hand in hand.

Smelling red roses and eating dishes that you would prepare.
Reading notes of love found in unlikely places to show that you care.

Talking on the phone, we would both fall asleep.
Comforting was the joy of your smile to dry my eyes when I would weep.

Being there for me, you would always have my back.
Enjoying life and having each other, there was not much to lack.

Holding me in your arms, I could feel your heart beat.
Waking to the sound of your voice, there was no better treat.

Snuggling in the bleachers, we cheered for our favorite team.
Spending an eternity together, that was our dream.

      I am remembering love and remembering you.

*Let your actions be the reason someone remember you,
when they remember love.*

Live life with valor

Two Hearts

We are like:

Two hearts beating as one,
Knowing our friendship has just begun.

Two hearts longing for each other,
Sharing a love with one another.

Two hearts singing a song for each to cherish,
Dreaming, hoping to never perish.

Two hearts bearing whatever comes our way,
Living and learning each and every day.

Two hearts filling up with love's treasure,
More than mere words could ever measure.

*If your actions show love,
Words will never measure the love someone will feel for you.*

LOVE, LIFE & COURAGE

Your Sweetness

The smell of a rose, the taste of nectar,
Cannot compare to your sweetness.

Your kindness, dreams, and desires,
Have become my very weaknesses.

I long for your touch and thirst for your kiss.
Just thinking of you puts me in a state of true bliss.

You have filled my life with color and so much more.
Like an eagle with wings, I am beginning to soar.

My dear, this is what you do to me.
It is your sweet love that makes my life complete.

Let your sweetness put someone in a state of true bliss.

J. B. LOVE

Live life with valor

My Everything

You are my everything,
Because of the joy you bring,

To me each and every day.
You chase my gray skies away.

You are a dream come true,
That makes me feel anew.

To hold you in my arms,
Feel heavenly with all your love and charm.

You are my everything,
Because of the happiness you keep sharing.

Be the joy that makes someone feel anew.

LOVE, LIFE & COURAGE

Safe Haven

When I am down and feeling blue,
I look to my heart and there I see you.

My heart gives me the courage that helps me make it through each day,
Because it is in my heart that my love for you can never be taken away.

My heart is my safe haven away from all my pain,
And you are the sun rays that wipes away the rain.

So, whenever I am feeling like I just cannot make it through,
I'll look to my heart because there is where I always find you.

Be the safe haven in someone's heart,
Because there your love will never part.

Live life with valor

Forbidden Love

Forbidden Love,
Never to be.
Two hearts,
Yearning for all the see.

Forbidden Love,
Never to be.
Two souls,
Searching for tranquility.

Forbidden Love,
Never to be.
Two lives,
Hoping for eternity.

Forbidden Love,
Never to be.
Two free spirits,
Fighting to make our love a reality.

At least once in a lifetime you will find a love worth fighting for.

LOVE, LIFE & COURAGE

Emotional Struggle

My heart says yes, but my mind says no.
Each speaks to me with their uncertainties.
I'm torn between the two.
It's eating at my very soul.
The fear of the unknown.

Once you face your fears, they will become history.

Live life with valor

You are the One

You are like the air that I breathe, all that I need, you complete me.
You are the reason that I live, my everything, the one for the world to see.

You are my dream come true, an angel on earth. I asked, and God sent me,
The perfect gift.
You are the joy my heart feels, the love of my life, and the one I want to,
Spend eternity with.

                              You are the one.

*Be the virtuous one God intended you to be
and the one for you will find you.*

LOVE, LIFE & COURAGE

Still

After all these years, I still enjoy looking at you.
You still warm my heart through and through.

You still fulfill all my desires.
Oh, how you set me on fire!

I still love the way you do the things you do.
Each day I still can't wait to come home because the spice feels so new.

I still look forward to spending an eternity with you and that's true.
Baby, I'm <u>Still</u> in love with you.

Be that person someone wants to spend eternity with.

Live life with valor

Inspiration

(A Tribute to a Legend)

You have a smile that is so infectious, it makes the sun rise in your eyes and,
Lights up the world around you.
You have provided a pathway for others to follow through.

Your charismatic ways are a reflection of your upbringing and platinum heart.
Regardless of any imperfection, you were an inspiration from the very start.

A legend like the world has never seen, you are more than a supernova for sure.
You show up when it counts the most and that has always provided the lure.

A bolt of lightning; you are amazing and your flavor is electrifying.
Greatness was always inevitable; there was just no denying.

You are simply beautiful like the stars shinning in the sky at night.
Always remember that in life only you can defeat you and like diamonds,
May your light forever shine bright.

A true child of destiny, the world loves you and is addicted to your light.
The wind will echo your name across the decades just like first sight.
The impact you have had on your sport, children in need and,
Others is immeasurable.
Where you go from here is your choice, thank you, it has been enjoyable.

*Keep Smiling! Smiles are infectious.
You never know whose life it will touch.
We unknowingly inspire by simply being ourselves.*

LOVE, LIFE & COURAGE

God's Love
(A Song of Love)

Verse 1
When I think of God's Love and <u>what He has done for me</u>.
It has brought me through trials and <u>made my life complete</u>.

When I thought it was over and <u>no one seem to care</u>.
He showed me through HIS love that He <u>always will be there</u>.

Chorus
Love, <u>God's Love,</u> I'm talking about God's love and <u>what He's done for me</u>.
Love, <u>God's Love,</u> I'm walking by faith because <u>He has set me free</u>.
Love, <u>God's Love,</u> I'm singing a new song and <u>praising His holy name</u>.
Love, <u>God's Love,</u> Since I found it, my life has <u>never been the same</u>.

Verse 2
Now I'm a testimony <u>living to tell the world</u>.
How great God's Love is, more precious than <u>diamonds or pearls</u>.

If you would allow him to <u>come into your heart</u>.
He will fulfill your desires if only you would <u>do your part</u>.

Chorus
Love, <u>God's Love,</u> I'm talking about God's love and <u>what He's done for me</u>.
Love, <u>God's Love,</u> I'm walking by faith because <u>He has set me free</u>.
Love, <u>God's Love,</u> I'm singing a new song and <u>praising His holy name</u>.
Love, <u>God's Love,</u> Since I found it, my life has <u>never been the same</u>.

Love, <u>God's Love,</u> I'm talking about God's love and <u>what He's done for me</u>.
Love, <u>God's Love,</u> I'm walking by faith because <u>He has set me free</u>.

God's love will make your life complete.

J. B. LOVE

Live life with valor

A Mother's Love is Always

There is so much to teach, yet so little time:

A mother's unconditional love is unselfish,
Always giving without reason.

A mother's love is rewarding,
Always watching over the fruits of her labor.

A mother love is constant,
Always instilling values that will last.

A mother's love is forever,
Always implanting in her child.

I have much love to give,
Because it was always given to me.

A mother's love is always and forever.

LOVE, LIFE & COURAGE

Reflections of Love
(A Tribute to Momma)

Waking to smell of breakfast, oh, what a treat.
Stories told by the fireside to warm our souls and feet.

Bandaging ouches, comforting fears and wiping our tears when we would cry.
Homemade ice cream, potato salad, cobbler, biscuits and fried chicken,
That was better than money could buy.

Images of great examples you gave to live our life by.
Dreams and hope for the future of success, encouraging us to always try.

These are my reflections of love.

Seek to be a reflection of love.

Live life with valor

Grateful Love
(A Grandmother Who Was Heaven Sent)

We are grateful to God for all the blessings to us He has sent.
But most of all, we are grateful to have had a grandmother like you,
With precious time we have spent.
Through the good examples you set, you have taught us that,
It is not what we acquire that will determine our true wealth,
But the choices we make in life that will not only determine our wealth but,
Will increase our spiritual health.
A pillar of the community you were and because of what you've shown,
generations will learn your legacy. Your teachings will be in vain never.
We will cherish your love and memory forever.

Thank You

Thank you for listening, all the times when I needed to share.
Thank you for raising a child with such tender love and care.
Thank you for your support when times were hard to bear.
Thank you for trying to find good in all life's evil and despair.
Thank you for your love and always being there.
Above all, thank you for your generosity,
A trait with which many cannot compare.

Always be grateful and thankful for your blessings.

LOVE, LIFE & COURAGE

Romance Departed

Once there was enough spice to fuel both our fires.
Your expression of the affection you felt met my desires.

Now apathy reigns and adventure and excitement have become,
Things of the past.
We are now searching for those feeling we both thought would last.

Gone is that space between anticipation and reality.
Lost in the bittersweet memory, we have now just exhausted all possibility.

There are pain and hurt in the acknowledgement.
Knowing that we have traded foreplay for what seems to be that,
We are just abstinent.

Not recognizing love anymore from what we started.
A new chapter has begun, and romance has utterly departed.

When romance departs, love soon follows.

J. B. LOVE

Live life with valor

Broken Promises of Love

I should have paid attention to the signs:

Craving yet starving,
Wanting yet needing,
Full yet filled with an empty and void feeling,
Hoping yet heart broken,
Hearing words yet actions are missing,
Wishing for a change yet the same is remaining,
Living yet dying,
Searching in the dark for light yet not finding,

Where are the reflections of love that were promised?

What's on the inside eventually surface and shows up on the outside. Pay attention to the signs.

Fellas all a real woman want is love (respect, affection & appreciation). Ladies if he loves you, you will not have to ask. If the signs are not there, don't waste your beauty & time. Keep it moving.

LOVE, LIFE & COURAGE

Learning to Love Me

My heart had to set you free,
So that I could learn to love me.

My mind had to let you go, you see,
So that I could be the best I could be.

With all of self-esteem's rewards for free,
The cost of loving you was too painfully.

I used to love you more than life itself, I couldn't see.
Now, I have finally learned to love me and I am finally free.

When you learn to love yourself, you make better choices in life.

The Magic in You

Magic mirror on the wall, I'm before you trying to stand tall.
As I start my day, I need some of your magic to protect me to meet its call.

Magic Mirror:
I'm only your reflection. The real magic is within you, there is no spell to install.
Before me I see a beautiful you capable of bringing joy and inspiration to all.
Keep the faith, work hard, love by giving to others and yourself and,
Short you will never fall.
You are a thousand times more resilient than any evil that could ever befall.

The magic needed to shine resides within you.

Live life with valor

Why I am Beautiful

I am beautiful because. . . . . ..

My spirit and my soul they radiate beauty.
I come from people that are as beautiful as they are diverse,
Regardless of any sorrow.
I come from a heritage that is rich with the triumph of overcoming,
Great obstacles in life, the achievements against all odds,
And hope for a brighter tomorrow.

As I travel on this journey called life, I reach out where hope has faded.
I'm not leaving anything to life's chances.
No matter what storms come my way, I remember who I am,
And press on in spite of my circumstances.

I love and believe in myself enough to empower others to become their,
Visions and to live their dreams because it makes the world better around me.
I want everyone know that they are beautiful also and can achieve.
They just need to look within their selves to find that prince, princess,
King or queen and only believe.

My heart is platinum, and I am always beautiful. I learned that was not new,
And guess what beautiful, so are you.

You become what you believe.

LOVE, LIFE & COURAGE

Beauty Undefined

What is Beauty?

Beauty can never be defined you see.
For it is in the eyes of the beholder, that's where true beauty resides and,
That's key.
So love and be your best self, because inside of everyone there is a beauty.
Therefore, you should behold yourself beautiful and believe.
Beauty is you and beauty is me.
It is living life to its fullest on your terms; that is true beauty.

It is unique, it is love, it is life and it is courage.

Behold yourself beautiful, believe, reflect it and just do you.

Live life with valor

Love Is

Love is . . .

Being there when it really counts,
Having someone's back and giving of your time in any amount.

The kindness from words you speak,
That warms hearts and breathes life into the souls of the meek.

Providing the care and support that is your duty.
Watching the growth from it, oh, can't you see all the beauty?

Love is forever and the way you make others feel,
That allows their desires and dreams to become real.

*Love is two hearts falling so that they can rise in love together as one.
Love is forever.*

LOVE, LIFE & COURAGE

Love is Not

Love is not . . .

Having to run someone down in the middle of the day or night.
Flowers and words of comfort after disrespect or abuse,
To make everything appear all right.
A big house, fancy car, fine jewelry, and clothes that are out of sight.
Keeping your mouth shut when you should speak and do what is right.
A reward for complying as it is forever and for this you should always fight.

Love should never hurt. If you ask for someone's heart and they give it to you, it's yours to protect and cherish not break; otherwise, you should not ask.

Too Educated to Quit

You can usually answer every question known contained in any book.
But you cannot explain why in the wrong places for a mate you continue to look.
You possess many degrees and that is a fact.
However, good common sense you seem to lack.
Somehow you think the criminal, abuser, leech or player is good catch.
Constantly searching for that inappropriate match.
You can go ahead, fess up and stop with the pretense.
Let us just face it, education without common sense is nonsense.

Education without common sense is nonsense.

Live life with valor

Love versus Lust

In lust, without regard for the consequences, people's mind seeks one thing only
After it's over *(the excitement of the chase and the acts)* here come the silence and,
You are assured to be left lonely.

In love, people's mind has each other best interest at heart.
Love filled hearts that seek to rise together and become one with each other;
A love that will rarely depart.

Sure they told you, "I Love You" but never showed you or told you "only".
Sure they spent one night, one month, six months or even a year;
Yet, while leaving behind the bittersweet memories, they left you lonely.

Sure they told their boys, you were amongst the baddest chicks.
They even bragged about all your skills and wonderful tricks;
Yet, when your heart fell, they left you lonely.

Sure they commanded your silence and told you they wanted to,
Keep things low-key.
Yet, they were posing in pics with someone else that ended up on social media,
For the world to see;
Now, they have moved on and you are still lonely.

Sure you stayed close to their mother;
Hoping one day they would tire of sowing their wild oats and,
Choose you over any other.
It's been a decade and you still talk from time to time; yet, you are still lonely.

LOVE, LIFE & COURAGE

Sure you tricked them to the altar,
Hoping they would change and discover a love that will never falter,
It's been years; yet, you are still lonely.

Sure you had their baby,
Hoping that one-day maybe.
Now they are standing at the altar with another and you are still lonely.

Love begets Love but Lust begets Loneliness. Choose Love Don't waste your beauty & time. Always remember the difference.

Win Big by Choosing Right

Rocky or smooth the paths on the roads of life we choose,
Always determines whether we win or lose.
Right, wrong or popular the decision is ours to make;
However, it takes more effort to clean up a mistake.
So make good choices and make them well.
If you choose the right path, you're sure to excel.

Every choice we make in life leads us to our destiny. What will your destiny be? Choose Right.

© J. B. Love

Live life with valor

Joy Comes in the Morning
(A Love Letter to My Heart)

Dear Heart,

I am compelled to write you this letter to let you know.
That I am taking over and it is time to let go.

I know it hurts now but it is only part of the process of growing.
There is a better life to live and it's all in the knowing.

You are beautiful beyond what you can now imagine.
To get you to hear my plea has become my passion.

Real love cannot be found where it does not exist.
If we wait too long, the opportunity will be missed.

A life of joy, happiness, and true love awaits you.
If only you would remember me, move on and be through.

Healing will come with each day the sun rises and sets.
I'll be here to guide and show you the way and that you can bet.

I Love You,

Your Mind

Healing comes with each day the sun rises and sets.

LOVE, LIFE & COURAGE

The Sun Shall Always Rise
(A Promise of Hope and Love)

My mind is full with so many thoughts.
I remember the good times of joy, happiness and the love you brought.

Yet, I remember the bad times and how they sometimes cut like a knife.
Not wanting to travel back down that road of constant strife.

Days, weeks and months all turned into years as time went by.
The tears I shed in the beginning as I went to sleep, I would cry.

Images of the times gone by are tearing at my very soul.
Coping with feelings of loneliness and losing control.

Waiting for that love to surface again, but finally realizing it's gone.
Making peace with my decision, I must leave those thoughts alone.

All those feelings are gone now as I await the joy that comes,
In the morning without surprise.
Remembering that with each dewdrop that falls, the sun shall always rise.

With each dewdrop that falls, the sun shall always rise.

J. B. LOVE

Live life with valor

Better
(An Opportunity to Spread Love)

So the doctor gave me a bitter cup of Java today to drink.
At first my mind was blown at a grave beckoning and I could barely think.

The thought of no more seasons began to eat at my very soul.
As gloom, despair, and silence began to take hold.

There were no words to convey all my fears.
As I search for answers of "why me" while trying to hold back the tears.

After the shock was over, I decided to take a proactive stance.
While trying to fight off naysayers who didn't know my story from a glance.

To some I became invisible as I took the time to heal.
My way would not have been their way.
Yet, in all my pain through a smile and kind words,
God showed me a glance of a brighter day.

I was once trampled by other's view of beauty, even race.
Gone now are those negative energies from my space.

Out of the ashes of despair, I emerged more beautiful now that I am,
Living life on my terms as I realized true beauty lies within the heart.
On the journey through life, I pay it forward by simply doing my part.

My fears have been put asunder and kingdom come will have to wait,
Because there is yet time for me to be great:

> To love better, to live better, and to be better.

Sometimes bad news is only the beginning of your destiny. Greatness is a choice. Love better, live better and be better and the rest will follow.

LOVE, LIFE & COURAGE

Unstoppable Love Share

Some of us have a heart that's platinum and filled with so much love.
Love that was given to us to share from above.
Yet, some of us wonder if "they" are aware.
Yet, some of us wonder if "they" even care.
Because of their negativity, I'm always aware.
If 'they" never acknowledge my goodness, I don't care.
Although of haters, we must always be aware.
Their hatred should never stop our heart's desire of endless love to share.

Don't let hatred stop your heart's desire to share love.

J. B. LOVE

Live life with valor

```
        L
    COURAGE
        V
      LIFE
```

LOVE, LIFE & COURAGE

Part 2: Life & Courage

Living
Involvement
Forever Changing
Eternal

Commitment
Opportunity
Using Valor
Rising
Action
Giving
Enduring

I have always used the above acronyms for life and courage. Life is about living and getting involved. It is forever changing, and I believe it is eternal. Even if you don't believe in "life after death," it is about the legacy you leave behind and the memories that will remain long after you are gone. My outlook on life has always been to live life it to its fullest on my terms. Just like success, living life to its fullest can only be defined by you. It's as I have always said, "not everyone wants to climb Mt. Everest". Courage is the one thing we all have within us to make this possible. Courage is about making a commitment and taking action when the opportunity presents itself. It is using valor *(personal bravery)* and rising after you have fallen. We all fall sometimes; however, it is how well we rise after falling that defines us. It is also about giving of yourself unselfishly and enduring the bitter storms of life. I hope that these poems of encouragement will invoke a sense of responsibility for you to have the courage to do the right things, to be true to who you are, to enjoy life, and to give of yourself unselfishly. After all, imagine what life would be like today if the many pioneers of change did not have the courage to invoke it. Dr. King once said, "I have a dream." I like to think that I live my dream

Live life with valor

```
        L
    COURAGE
        V
      LIFE
```

LOVE, LIFE & COURAGE

each and every day, and that is very real. Our dreams can and do become realities with the right actions, dedication, and perseverance in life.

What does it mean to do the right thing? First, from my experiences and observations, I can tell you that it means having the courage to be true to who you are as a person, to love yourself, to do what is right for you, and to rid your space of negativity. Don't let others dictate to you who you are and destroy your self-esteem and happiness. Learn to love who you are so that you can begin to share that love with the world around you. Sometimes in life, you have to march to the beat of a different drum. You can spend a lifetime trying to make someone love and appreciate you to no avail. Just think about it. When was the last time you spent too much time attempting to get others to accept you, love you, and respect you? Now think about what you could have done with that time. If people don't let you shine in their arena, sometimes you have to find an arena you can shine in or better yet, create your own park. Often, you need to rid your space of negativity. As talked about earlier, you will never be able to shine with negativity in your space. There is too much haze. Negative people and environments are like weeds in your flower garden of life. If you allow the weeds to remain, they will overtake your life, and you will never receive the valuable nourishment needed to grow and prosper.

Second, doing the right things also mean having the courage to stand up for what is right, to speak out against that which is unjust, and to share love equally. It is the courage to help others, especially taking a risk to help children who are usually not in a position to help themselves. You should never be a fence rider. Fence riders never want to make waves. They sit on top of their fences and pretend not to see what is going on. They continue to keep their eyes, mind and mouth shut to the wrong things that are going on around them or they put their selves in the middle becoming part of the problem only making matters worse. Other people are being destroyed and hurt. In the end, people will have more respect for you if you have the courage to make a difference. It might just save someone's life. You should always share love equally. Just because a person is a particular race, it does not automatically make them more or less than anyone else. You should treat all people with love and respect. You cannot confine beauty to individual races. Crazy, ignorance and an ugly heart are universal and knows no color. Let's turn the pages and take a look at my experiences and observations of life and courage on my journey through life.

Live life with valor

Life in Motion

Listen to the echoes of life's memories.

Hear the sweet sounds of life's melodies.

Feel the love of life's opportunities.

See the signs of life's journeys.

Taste the success of life's victories.

Redo, and live life to its fullest on your terms and fulfil your destiny.

Life is always in motions, beckoning us to hop aboard and enjoy the ride. Live life to its fullest on your terms.

LOVE, LIFE & COURAGE

The Cycle of Life
(Born to Live)

Creating,
Arriving,
Observing,
Acting,
Loving,
Struggling,
Winning,
Sinking,
Escaping,
Rising,
Thriving,
Living,
Dying,
Yet Living.

Only those who believe that there is no life after death believe that they were born to die.

Live life with valor

To Live or Not

To truly live or not to live, this should be the question.

Will you choose to be all that you can be, or will you choose to only exist,
Living life without any challenges and never taking any risks?

Will you rise each day only to lie down and shut your eyes for tomorrow,
Always living for yesterday, wallowing in all its splendor and sorrow?

Will you stop to thank your higher being for making all things possible,
Or will you attribute everything to chance, thinking without it no man is,
Capable?

Will you try to make life better not only for you but for all mankind,
Or will you continue to live for self, always crying me, my, mine?

Will you stop to notice all the beauties that life offers,
Or will you live life with blinders on, ignoring nature's splendid wonders?

To be should never be your only vision, can't you see.
For to truly live life to its fullest on your terms is far better than just to be.

To live or not? Let your actions be your answer.

LOVE, LIFE & COURAGE

Life is Like a Poem

Life is like a poem of never ending versus,
Of words not yet written and lines not yet rehearsed.

Each day we live our lives there is a story to be told,
Captured in the imagination of a poet, and written for all to behold.

Have you ever thought about what your life will be?
Was it designed to create one harmonious symphony?

Will it be an epigram, over before it has begun,
Or will it be a lyric, left to sing your life's song?

Will it be a sonnet, short lived in all its glory,
Or will it be an elegy; after you're gone that truly narrates your life story?

Be your best self and make your life's story great.

Rhymed or unrhymed, life comes in many forms,
What you call experiences and observances, we poets call poems.

J. B. LOVE

Live life with valor

Courage Is

Courage is...

Standing tall,
When your back is against the wall.

Speaking out against that which is unjust when it's not popular to do so.
The one thing in life that will always allow you to grow.

Venturing out of your comfort zone in spite of danger, fear or pain.
Being yourself knowing that there is always sunshine after the rain.

Be courageous, it will allow you to grow.

LOVE, LIFE & COURAGE

The Courage to Rise

In spite of all your fears,
Rise!

In spite of all the tears,
Rise!

In spite of all the wasted years,
Rise!

When the way is not always clear,
Rise!

When it appears that the end is drawing near,
Rise!

For all that you hold dear,
Rise!

Courage will give you the power to,
 RISE!

You will always be defined by how well you rise after falling down.

Live life with valor

The Courage to Begin

The highways of my mind are taking me to places that I never been.

Vision of success along life's journey have become my best friend.

Belief in myself will be a win, win.

Effort will determine in the end.

Change will not occur unless I take different actions and begin.

Change will not occur without different actions and beginning.

LOVE, LIFE & COURAGE

The Courage to Live

Faith gives me to courage to live life to its fullest on my terms . . .

I'm throwing caution to the wind.

Rewards will be great; it's just a matter of when.

Adventure always leads to fulfillment in the end.

It's about now not then.

Hope resides deep within.

Determination and effort will bring success again and again.

Faith gives me the courage to seek and obtain my happiness, live and win.

Have the courage to seek and live your happiness.

Live life with valor

Daybreak

(A Chance to Start Out New)

Hues of yellow and red, mingled with shades of blue,
Rising above the horizon, ushering in the light of a day with,
A chance to start out new.

After the dawn chorus whispers melodies of sounds so sweet and tender.
Sunrise, sunshine looks so good in all its splendor.

Oh, the smell of dew droplets still on the grass and flowers,
I can't wait to awake,
Because there is nothing quite as beautiful as daybreak.

Each daybreak always brings with it the opportunity to start out new.

LOVE, LIFE & COURAGE

Paradise

Drifting on the crystalline, turquoise waters of the Caribbean Sea,
Of the Atlantic Ocean,
Enchanting are the feelings and just one of life's little adventures in motion.

Basking in the radiant, warm rays of California's Sun.
Playing volley ball on the beach, I'm just having fun.

Resting by the warm fireplace on a cashmere rug in the Colorado Mountains.
Creating angels in the snow, I'm just enjoying life's youthful fountains.

Eating succulent, fresh seafood on Florida's Coast.
Being with that special one is tranquility and what I love the most.

Enjoying paradise is wherever I am. It doesn't matter where in the world,
My journeys land.
Making life serene should be your goal by making wherever you are grand.

Don't make life miserable by not appreciating what you have.
Paradise is wherever you are if you make it so.

Live life with valor

Remembering When
(A Tribute to Grandma)

I am remembering life and love . . .

When I was young, life seemed so carefree.
Strolling through the woods to my grandparent's old place,
Picking fruit from a tree.

Sitting on the porch escaping the scorching sun.
Playing with siblings, cousins and neighboring kids, just having fun.

Dipping our feet in the water from the pond's bank.
Drinking rain fallen cool water from grandma's tank.

Traveling on narrow gravel dusty roads.
Watching families gather crops by the truckloads.

Trips to the airport on Sundays after church to watch planes take off and land.
Vacationing on the gulf coast walking along the beach, barefoot in the sand.

Listening to the sounds of the time played on the radio all day.
Getting by on what we had because our parents always made a way.

Sipping fresh squeeze lemonade and tea to quench our thirst.
Racing to eat fresh picked cucumber and tomatoes from grandma's garden first.

Learning to ride my first bicycle without training wheels, my first crush and kiss.
Wanting to be all grown up was sometimes my wish.

LOVE, LIFE & COURAGE

Walking and talking with love ones gone by.
Sometimes now I miss them and want to cry.

Like Grandma used to say sometimes when it rained it would pour,
But there was always comfort in knowing,
Opportunity was just around the corner to open its door.

How unjust things were for some people and wondering why.
Wishing for a time when all would enjoy equality, even I.

Day dreaming about the future and the possibility.
Wondering where I would end up and what would be my reality.

This is now and that was then.
Yet, I still remember when.

When you build lasting memories, your legacy will live on.

Live life with valor

I Say

Some say I am opinionated and everyone has one.
Others say I think I know it all and act as if I am better than some.

I say my mind is unique with the ability to think, to reason, and to decide.
Unafraid to speak out against that, which is unjust. That is where I get my pride.

I say I strive to be all that my mind can imagine.
I'm driven by a consciousness that is fair and has compassion.

I say I know all of what it is that I know.
I'm always constantly seeking to learn more.

People will say what they will say, but that will not stop me.
A beautiful young mind continuously reaching to be all that it can be.

You are always what you say and believe.
If you allow others to stop you, you become just like them.

Driven by their thoughts, some people's words and actions lack knowledge and intelligence and don't deserve your time.
The wise ignore and keep moving forward.

If people won't let you shine in their arena, find another, better yet, create your own.

LOVE, LIFE & COURAGE

A Mind of Many Colors

My mind is of many colors each shade is unique.
Like a box of crayons, when put together this makes my mind set complete.

Yellow to represent the sun's light, each day I will rise for anew.
Red to represent fire, a smile for all, to warm them through and through.

Purple to represent the heart, courageous and kind in all my deeds.
Brown to represent the earth, to carefully plant my seeds.

Blue to represent the sky, to reach for the unlimited,
Orange to represent fruit, to produce when times are rigid.

Green to represent grass, with places for my mind to roam around.
Black and White to represent music, to appreciate all life's wonderful sounds.

With my mind of many colors, the world is my open canvas and,
I am the artist for all to see,
As I continue to reach for the stars, to paint my world a masterpiece.

Make the world your open canvas & paint it a masterpiece.

Embrace Yourself, Uniqueness, Dreams, Preparation, Action, Success & Repeat. It's the Only Way to Grow.

Live life with valor

One Sistah's Cry

Why can't you appreciate me for all that I am worth?
After all, it was from me that you were given birth.

By your choices, you often dissociate yourself from me,
By choosing only what surface sake will allow you to see.

Don't you know that I am beautiful within my own right.
It has been for this very cause that it has always been a continuous fight.

My hair is of many lengths and textures; my face is of many shades of coloring,
But my heart is saddened, that you find me so unflattering.

Not able to see beauty anymore from your deep melancholy vision.
A quintessential man who's headed for a belief and truth collision.

People are different, but because of racism, to you, I am now a stereotype.
Nevertheless, I'm beholding beauty and forgetting all the exaggerated hype.

Because yours is a belief system that destined to falter.
Can't you see that I am a walking, talking testament of all I have to offer?

Share Love Equally. Beauty is not confined to certain races. Crazy, ignorance and an ugly heart are universal and knows no color.

LOVE, LIFE & COURAGE

My Essence

You will not stop me with all your distractions.
The essence of who I am, is not determined by your actions.

You will not silence me with your slander!
My mellifluous character will out shine any propaganda.

You will not run me away with your threats!
I'm living my life on my terms, I have no regrets.

You will not slay me with your passion.
My will is stronger than you can imagine.

Who you are should only be determined by you.

Live life with valor

Fence Riders

Look at all the fence riders, perched high upon their fences.
They're trying not to get involved for fear of getting caught in the trenches.

If only they would realize, that in the trenches they will find courage and growth.
Not only for the other person but also for both.

Don't be a fence rider, get involved and make a difference.

LOVE, LIFE & COURAGE

A Fair-Weather Friend

Beware of a fair-weather friend.
They are not genuine, although they will pretend,
They are never there for you in the end.
When the weather is fair, oh they will contend.
Let one drop of rain fall and they are gone like the wind.
Over backwards they will never bend.
Even though they have taken from you time and time again,
They are not real and usually have nothing to lend.

Beware, Beware of a Fair-Weather Friend

Real friends are hard to come by. Share love with and cherish them.

Modified Serenity Prayer

Grant me the serenity to accept the fact that I cannot change others,
The courage to change those things I can,
That I want to see within myself and,
The wisdom to recognize with whom my time is better spent,
That will make all the difference.

You cannot change others.
Don't waste time. Keep it moving.
The only person you can change is yourself.

J. B. LOVE

Live life with valor

A Vow of Silence

A vow of silence will not let some do what is right.
The wicked things they hear and see are always out of mind, out of sight.

It has imprisoned them into thinking that one voice will never be heard.
Therefore, they keep their minds closed and never utter a single word.

Not realizing that in their silence they have become an accessory,
To the very things they hear and see.

They sometimes choose a path that they feel is safe,
Until it hits home and threatened their own sacred place.

Now it will be forever implanted in their very soul.
Things that would have never happened if long ago they had only told.

Speak up. Silence is the catalyst for continued violence.

LOVE, LIFE & COURAGE

In the Middle

Are we always caught in the middle,
Or do we tend to always put ourselves there?
We come to the table loudly with no solution in sight anywhere.

We jump up and down and scream that we are not the blame.
Even though our intentions were always to seek fame.

Is it unfair to be at this place at this time,
Or is it punishment for our actions, that only fit the crime?

Be a part of the solution not the problem.
If you can't bring a solution to the table, stay away or
at least keep quite.

J. B. LOVE

Live life with valor

Why Bother

Why do you ask me my opinion when that is not what you want to hear?
Is it the thought of the truth that you have come to fear?

Why do you ask me how I am doing when you do not care?
If you're only asking for politeness sake, then why even dare.

So I could wear a mask and wear it well,
If there is ever anything wrong, you will never be able to tell.

So when you ask how I'm doing, I could say just fine and you.
When you ask me what I think, I could reply whatever you think, will do.
However, would that not make me fake just like you, boo?

After all, we both know that's not what you want.
You could have saved us both the trouble by not wasting both our time,
And been honest up front.

*If you are sincere and honest with people,
they will be sincere and honest with you.*

LOVE, LIFE & COURAGE

Who am I?

Some say I do not exist and I am a thing of the past.
But if you would only open your heart and eyes, you can remember where and,
When you saw me last.

I helped imprison minds into thinking they were more and less,
And most of you probably think you have seen me at my best.

I have made mankind's heart turn to stone,
With new generations, come more souls for me to clone.

I left behind me a legacy filled with blood and pain.
I tell you today that if you do not stop me, the future will only hold the same.

You know me as racism, but if the truth is told,
I am a living cancer that will continue to spread,
Unless you acknowledge my existence and put an end to all my dread.

Racism is a living cancer that will continue to spread unless we acknowledge its existence and put an end to all its dread.

Live life with valor

Bless the Little Children

God bless the little children who are helpless and without a care,
Who look to us for our love, if only we would share.

God bless the little children who depend on us for their welfare,
Who look to us for guidance, just knowing that we will always be there.

God bless the little children who are in this world alone,
Who look to us for shelter, to provide them with a safe and nurturing home.

God bless the little children who parents have gone astray,
Who look to us as positive role models, praying not to end up the same way.

God bless the little children who suffer pain and abuse,
Who look to us for refuge to save them for the accused.

God bless the little children who will grow up to have children of their own,
Who will look to you for their strength, to enable them not to do wrong.

Children are a blessing and should be treated as one.

LOVE, LIFE & COURAGE

Because of You
(A Child's Plea)

If you teach me, I will know,
All the thing in life I need to grow.

If I watch you, I will learn,
The choices to make and paths to take when it is my turn.

If you nurture, love and support me,
The possibilities in life will be easier for me to see.

What I become in life will be in part because of you.

*Be a positive role model in a child's life,
they are watching and learning.*

J. B. LOVE

Live life with valor

I See, I Hear, I Do

As I travel through life **I see** the wonderful possibilities.
I hear the sounds of success, calling me and tempting me with opportunities.
I have the courage to be me and **I do** the best using my abilities.

I See, I Hear, I Do
When opportunity knocks, will you hear?

Grind to Shine
(Survival is Everything)

"Every day in the world, a mogul wake up. He/she knows they must outperform the fastest growing competition or be overtaken. Every day in the world, the competition wakes up. They know they must grind quicker than the slowest growing mogul, or they will not survive. It doesn't matter whether you're the mogul or the competition. When the sun rises, you'd better be grinding if you want to survive and shine."

Never Become Too Complacent
© J. B. Love

LOVE, LIFE & COURAGE

Move, Grove and Be You

You got to keep moving, moving.

You got to keep grooving, grooving.

Don't worry about those who seem to hate you so.

They're just trying to wreck your flow.

Your smile, your walk, your talk, your thoughts and your glow.

Your best is what you should always show.

Being you will serve you well and it is all in the know.

Just Do You!

Live life with valor

Change Begins with Me

When I woke up each morning,
A new day was dawning.

Troubles had bound me and my tears had almost drowned me.
Fear had blocked me and doubt of overcoming had stopped me.
There was no way out that I could see.

My heart was hardening.
For a change I was yearning.

So I looked toward the heavens to pray,
That change would somehow come my way.

And then I discovered me. Now I wake up each morning,
and a new day is still dawning.

But hope now surrounds me.
I'm striving to be the best that I can be.

Each day I keep learning,
To continue striving and praying.

For joy to continue to come my way.
Now each tomorrow is a brighter day.

LOVE, LIFE & COURAGE

Because I learned that change begins with me, I'm . . .
Free from the troubles that bound me,
Free from the tears that drowned me,
Free from the fears that blocked me,
Free from the doubt that stopped me,
I'm Free, Finally Free, all because I learned to say yes to me.

Say yes to you! If someone is not adding value to who you are, rid your space of negativity.

Be a Blessing Everyday

Begin each day with:

Love in your heart as "love begets love"

Expectations of blessings abundantly

Sharing & spreading love, peace, & hope as goodness will follow

Smiling & shine like the sun to light up the world around you

Inspiring & empowering others to make the world a better place

Never forgetting to behold yourself beautiful and reflect it

Good thoughts on your mind as "good begets good"

If you can't be a blessing to someone, just keep it moving. Blessed are they that are a blessing to others.

Live life with valor

Encouraged

Be encouraged and stay blessed,
When life's troubles put you to the test.

Be encouraged and stay blessed.
Rise above the Naysayers and the rest.

Be encourage and stay blessed.
Always seek to give your very best.

Be encouraged and stay blessed.
Walk in the truth, a lie must be dressed.

It is easier to walk in the truth. Integrity separates you from the competition. Unethical has to be dressed.
Stay Encouraged and Forever Blessed

LOVE, LIFE & COURAGE

The House of They

On any street anywhere in the Valley of the Nays,
You can be assured to find a "Circle of Them" that resides in,
"The House of They".

Where people are spreading their gospel as the truth and the only way.
"They" have traded sharing love for spreading lies because,
That's all "they" know and their goal is always to lead you astray.
Always remember, "Who are "they" anyway?"
There actions are not unique and true meaning do "they" convey.
The only real power "they" possess is what you give away.
"They" rarely mean you any good on any given day.

"They" can't see your vision and negativity is the only thing,
"They" know how to portray.
Naysayers will become your footstools if you just remember to,
Ignore and keep them at bay.

Life should be about the discovery of "what is" and,
What "you" have to say.
Never let a small mind dictate as "they" do not contribute and,
"They" are only trying to betray.

Keep your head up, have faith, determination, courage and pray,
For this will give you the power to rise, stand, and stay.

Make your Naysayers stepping stones to something great.
Avoid the Valley of the Nays:
Nay Seers, Nay Doers & Naysayers

J. B. LOVE

Live life with valor

```
        L
COURAGE
        V
   LIFE
```

LOVE, LIFE & COURAGE

Conclusion

In conclusion, there is a biblical quote taken from the King James Version of the Bible in Luke, Chapter 12, verse 48 that many speakers have used and revised that reads, *for unto whomsoever much is given, of him shall be much required.* Life is about living and getting involved. It is giving, sharing love, having the courage to be yourself, speaking up for that which is unjust even when it is unpopular to do so, and making a difference in the lives of others and the world. If you have only been living for yourself thinking that the gifts you have obtained in life are only for yourself, your world must be tiny, lonely, and closing in on you daily. You should always choose to make a difference. It will make you a better you. It will empower others, improve the world around you, and just may save someone's life. Most of all you need to stop listening to what "they" say. Driven by their thoughts, some people's words and actions lack knowledge and intelligence. Haters do not deserve your time or attention, and small minds will never be able to see your visions. Don't worry, if it seems as though you are a misfit. Keep moving forward as God has something bigger and better in life for you. It is always about what you know and what you say that should determine your path in life. You should always share love, live life on your terms as though you are always drinking from the finest crystal glass daily, and have courage. Valor will allow you to do these things. Until next time, fill your life with love and peace and happiness will always follow. Be sure to check out my book, *How to Find, Enjoy and Keep Real Love (A Common Sense Guide to a Healthy Relationship)*, that I wrote based on the poems in this book. Stay blessed and encouraged. Follow me on Twitter: MuchLoveFromJLove @ForeverLove4All.

A Hater's Prayer

Lord, thank you for all that I am and,
For giving me the wisdom not to allow my haters to alter my self-worth.
They know not how to love.
Touch their hearts so that they too may enjoy happiness and spread love. Amen

www.ingramcontent.com/pod-product-compliance
Lightning Source LLC
LaVergne TN
LVHW051528070426
835507LV00023B/3359